For Tony Colwell, who spent so much more than eighty days on this book

To cover 24 countries in 96 pages is an almost impossible task. This is a book of hasty impressions gathered sometimes under adverse conditions. It records simply how the world looked to me in eighty days. Many people helped to make the journey pleasurable and I could not name them all here. But I would like to offer my special thanks to John Okinda the Kenyan driver who dragged me from the edge of a pool known to be the haunt of man-eating crocodiles, and to John Hall in New Zealand for an exhilarating afternoon spent rolling giant boulders into a deep ravine. For travel expertise no one I met was more charmingly efficient than Marilyn Hall at the Cyprus Hilton. My thanks also to the French courier on the Orient Express, who fed me with onion soup from his primus stove when I discovered the restaurant car had been taken off, and to the drivers who allowed me to sneak on to the 'footplate' of the Canadian Pacific. Above all, my warm regards to the hotel porter in Tokyo who politely handed back my tip.

John Burningham
London, 1972

Around the World in
EIGHTY DAYS

John Burningham

Around the World in
EIGHTY DAYS

Jonathan Cape ... ... re London

By the same author:

BORKA
TRUBLOFF
A B C
HUMBERT
CANNONBALL SIMP
HARQUIN
SEASONS
MR GUMPY'S OUTING

First published in 1972
© 1972 by John Burningham
ISBN 0 224 00659 2
Printed in Great Britain by Jarrold & Son Ltd, Norwich
Layout & title page design by Jan Pienkowski

On October 2nd, 1872, Jules Verne's hero, Phileas Fogg, set out from the Reform Club in London to travel round the world in 80 days. His trip was imaginary. Almost a hundred years later, on October 3rd,1970, I set out from the same address. Mine was quite real.

Well, at least I'm starting with a good English breakfast.

10.30 a.m. Golden Arrow, Victoria. I'm really off. All the months
of planning, and this is it: 28 flights, days and nights of trains,
cars and crocodiles lie ahead...Do I really need all this luggage?
At least a third of it seems to be taken up with bundles of tickets
I collected from Cook's only yesterday. Shall I ever get back?
Already I've nearly missed the boat at Dover.

Paris. Far too early at the Gare de l'Est. Orient Express pulls out at midnight. This train has been running since 1883. First run was also on October 4th.

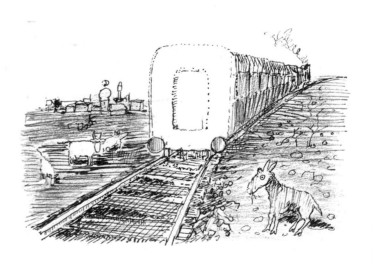

8

Three days and the train splits somewhere – where? Where?
Venice? Trieste? Belgrade? Sofia...? Nearly lost it altogether
nipping off for a sandwich at the Bulgarian border.

TURKEY
TÜRKİYE

Tuesday, October 6. Noon and Istanbul...a very big place to be in on one's own. I'll take a guided tour. I take one but am no less alone. A relief to fly off to Nicosia.

CYPRUS
ΚΥΠΡΟΣ

Afternoon tea with retired English colonels. Ride through a
mountain village on a plump donkey. Buy ticket from an armed
guard to see Turkish Cypriot fortified stronghold, once the fairy
castle Disney copied for Snow White film.

Aphrodite. The Templars, Richard the Lionheart, the British army...
This place has been a stopover for armies throughout history.

14

Amazes me how they ever moved on again.
Not sure I can.
And this is only the beginning.

15

EGYPT
مصر

October 13. Morning. Plane circles over Cairo. Where are the Pyramids? Never seen so many guns and missiles.

Return from camel ride. Nile prawns for dinner.

18

Next morning in bazaar: noise and damp heat and steamy eastern smells. Bed early, up again soon after midnight to catch 3 a.m. plane for Ethiopia before dawn mists settle over Nile.

ETHIOPIA
ኢትዮጵያ

October 15. Addis Ababa.

The air is fresh (almost 8,000 feet above sea level) and the clouds seem very near. Coloured umbrellas, palatial hotels and corrugated shacks.

Spend too much time trying to organize the bit of my ticket taken in error at Cairo.

21

KENYA

24

Sunday, October 18. Arrive at Nairobi. Land-Rover waiting with driver and guide. Six days of my own personal safari.

Bump away into a country varying from lush, wet, English greenery to hot, dusty plains with giraffe. If someone else does this trip in another hundred years, will there be any animals left I wonder?

Young bull elephants like to prove their strength

they have pushed the trees

they have to find a tree to stand under

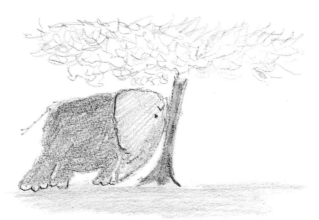 

by pushing over small trees. The trouble is that when

over and the hot sun shines on them

which probably has lots of other elephants under it
all trying to get out of the sun.

TREE TOPS HOTEL

At Malindi, near Mombasa, there is a remarkable marine national park along 3 miles of coast. No fishing or taking coral is allowed. All kinds of inquisitive fish swim up to see what people look like.

October 27. Night flight to Bombay via Karachi. Transistor radios keep me awake. Doze at last – and miss my breakfast. Worried about early morning connection to Aurangabad. A mad rush, but just make it.

36

INDIA
भारत

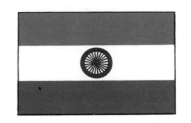

Plane lands on grass at Aurangabad. Taken to visit temples through a haze of exhaustion. Pity, but can't face cave paintings. Bed at last and another bad night: forgot to switch on fan and visited by mosquitoes through a hole in the net.

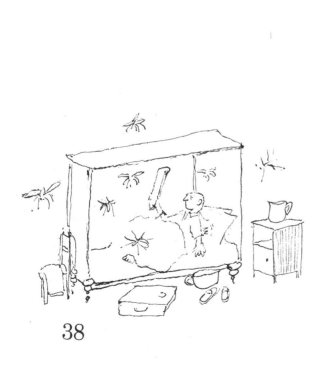

39

A land of more than 5,000 years of civilization. People seem to take no account of time and I rush past as in a dream.

On to Delhi. Hurry…Train to Agra and the Taj Mahal –
astonishing at midday, must be unbelievable by moonlight.

Return to Delhi for plane to Kathmandu.

NEPAL
नपाल

3 a.m. drive up perilous track to see Mount Everest at dawn.
But it's still fifty miles away. Back into India...

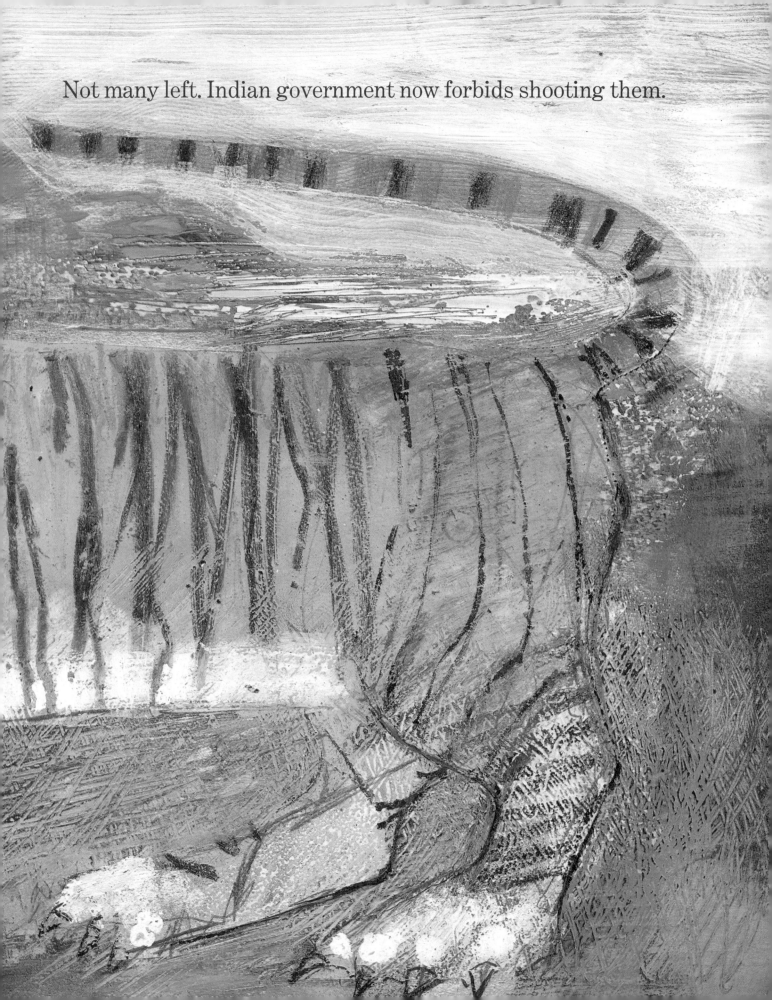

Not many left. Indian government now forbids shooting them.

48

Calcutta. The first Imperial capital and my last day in India.

November 6. Dum Dum Airport, Calcutta, and jet to Bangkok.

THAILAND
ประเทศไทย

Bangkok. Enormous outboard motors now career through this city of waterways. Odd place to narrowly escape a roasting when nightclub catches fire.

HONG KONG

Three nights in one place. Can it be true? Or should I be
somewhere else? There's an elaborate itinerary for tomorrow
(Sunday) morning. I revolt. I'm staying in bed. Can watch them
playing cricket from my window.

55

There are 17,000 junks in Hong Kong.
78,994 people live on boats of one kind or another.

57

JAPAN
日本

13.00 hrs. Tuesday, November 10, flight 274 on time at Tokyo.
Rush round the sights. Must catch Hikari 130 m.p.h. train to Kyoto.
Slept past Mount Fuji. Kyoto's shrines and gardens strangely
untouched by modern industrial Japan.

Could not leave without being boiled and pummelled in a traditional Japanese bath. I lay too long contemplating the Japanese art of arrangement – not just flowers but everything. Nearly miss the plane to Australia.

AUSTRALIA

November 15. Arrive tropical Darwin 4.30 in the morning.

Sprayed with insecticide. Now I know how it feels to be a wasp.

64

Clammy Sunday. No papers. No café. Only the Salvation Army
playing outside Woolworth's to three aborigines and me.

Want to drive across the desert to Sydney 2,000 miles south-east. Can't spare a week so it has to be another jet. This country's too vast to touch in the time. 32 times the size of the British Isles, with more sheep and cattle than people and the most modern opera house in the world.

NEW ZEALAND AOTEAROA

(Land of the Long White Cloud)

68

Arrive Christchurch 5.30 p.m. after adjusting to local time.
It's spring again. Oaks and green grass.
My farthest point. How odd to cross the world
and find things just the same. Public schools, bagpipes:
it could be a small town in Scotland.

Across the Alps and then ferry to the North Island and
Wellington. Plane to Rotorua left me dozing in Palmerston
North minus some luggage.

Fail to hitch-hike and end up hiring a car. Not sure what I would find when I visited the hot, sulphurous, bubbling mud springs of Rotorua at sunrise.

November 26. Catch up luggage in Auckland and embark on
S.S. Tofua. Three days' voyage to Fiji.

A rare albatross (symbol of good luck at sea) swoops low over the
ship. Alas, the Pacific rolls under a grey sky.

FIJI
VITI

It is raining on my island in the sun. Dripping palms. Money has
become like damp lettuce leaves. Taxi-driver told me about a
man who could walk into the sea and call the fish to him.
But not today.

Hop across to Tonga. The Friendly Islands, where people give
you presents in the streets.

TONGA

The tortoise Captain Cook gave to the Tongan Royal Family in 1774 died a few years ago. When a Tongan marries, he is given 7 acres of land to live on. The total area of the islands is only 270 square miles.

Back to Fiji, and taxi 180 miles across island to pick up weekly
Qantas flight to Mexico City. If we have a breakdown I'll be
stranded. But all's well, and I'm off 6,000 miles across the Pacific.
Half an hour in Tahiti. Cross International Date Line
and Equator. This means that tomorrow when we get there it
will be today all over again, or something like that.

MEXICO
MÉXICO

La Basílica de Guadalupe
MEXICO CITY 5/12/70.

December 6. Plane takes a long time to get airborne at Mexico
City because of the thin air so high in the mountains.
Los Angeles thick with a vast, grey, smoke haze. Straight on to
Grand Canyon.

Breathtaking descent into Canyon by mule.
Numb with cold and fright.

On to Flagstaff, where American astronauts train because the landscape is so like the surface of the moon.

Distances mean little here. Hire car and drive 300 miles into Indian territory. Cross the Arizona desert by bus in 12 hours. Everything is speeding up again.

90

91

San Francisco, then bus again through the **night, north** to Vancouver B.C.

92

CANADA

FLIGHT 216   TEL AVIV VIA JAMAICA   DELAYED
FLIGHT 412   MOSCOW PRAGUE VIA CEIN   GATE 9
FLIGHT 219   TOKYO. Now BOARDING   GATE 3
FLIGHT 876   LAS VEGAS   GATE 21
FLIGHT 944   DENVER AND L.A. ·
FLIGHT 216   MONTREAL
FLIGHT 999   LONDON · · · · · ·   DELAYED
FLIGHT 618   PARIS ROME ATHENS.

December 14. Canada rushes by – the Rocky Mountains…
Toronto…Niagara Falls…I'm nearly home.
Reach New York on the 20th. Held up by a last-minute airport
strike. Am I to be beaten after all by Phileas Fogg?

December 21. The eightieth day. And it's good to be back.
Perhaps I should have gone on the Trans-Siberian railway to
Peking and then across the Antarctic to…

Length of journey: 44,000 miles

Time taken: 80 days

Countries visited: France, Switzerland, Italy, Yugoslavia, Bulgaria, Turkey,
Cyprus, Egypt, Ethiopia, Kenya, Pakistan, India, Nepal, Thailand,
Hong Kong, Japan, Australia, New Zealand, Fiji, Tonga, Tahiti, Mexico,
the United States and Canada

Timetable arrangements: Thos Cook and Son, London.
It was also in 1872 that Mr Thomas Cook the first completed his first
world tour, although it took him 200 days: he contributed regular
despatches to The Times in London.

Other facilities generously provided by Qantas Airlines, Cyprus Airways,
British Railways, Canadian Pacific Railways, the P & O Steam Navigation
Company, Greyhound International, Kenya Tourist Office,
India Government Tourist Office, and Hilton International.

THOS. COOK & SON, LTD.
RESERVATIONS DEPT.
17 SEP 1970
BERKELEY STREET,
LONDON W1A 1EB.

奈里魚鹽

五百円
日本銀行券
日本銀行

500

500

Cette carte
le contrôle
attente. v...
blement. N...

Diese Ka
Kontroll
Ihnen
Wir au...
auszu...

EC

2 Nom de
Mädchenn...
3 Prénoms
Vornamer...
4 Date de n...
Geburtsda...
5 Lieu de n...
Geburtsor...
...tionali...
...atsange...
...rofession
Beruf - Oc...
8 Domicile
Adresse —
9 Durée du
Dauer de...
10 Poste fror
Grenzüberg...

Servicio en el mismo día si entrega
su ropa antes de las 11 a. m.

Same d...
deliver...

HOTEL MAJE...
México 1, D. F.
...DE LAVAND...
...UNDRY LIST

FIJI IMMIGRATION ORDINANCE
Sec. (9) and Regulation (10)
Date of entry 3. 12. 70
Entered as a visitor under
the provisions of section 9
Permitted to remain until
4. 12. 70

VISAS

ROYAL NEPALESE EMBASSY
LONDON

COAT OF ARMS
E II R
...KONG $1

FAMILY PLANNING
HCG INDIA

Visa granted at

THE ROYAL NEPALESE EMB...

Good for Single journey to Nep...
Six months of this date and ...
visit to Kathmandu, Pokhara an...
only for Two weeks from th...
entry if passport remains v...

No. ...70.38...
Date 24 / 9 / 70
RECEIVED 15/- FOR VISA

FARE
PAID
CLASS
STAGE
5 ORD 17
LONDON
TRANSPORT

ET...
...LINES...

BUS TICKET
One-Way Fare
EG£ 0.200
FORM BT/071 PAD

Tear both
if required

NEW ZEALAND
WELLINGTON
30c
Tongariro National Park

WAN...
ON THE W...

Cheque
Cash
Discount
Total
$ 3.00

With Thanks
ROTOKAWA THERMAL
...MOTEL
Per...

SEÑORES		RATE	GENTLEMEN
CAMISAS		4.00	SHIRTS
CAMISAS ALMIDONADAS		6.00	Shirts, Starched
CUELLOS		2.00	COLLARS
CAMISETAS		2.00	UNDERSHIRTS
CALZONCILLOS		3.00	DRAWERS
UNIDOS		5.00	Union Shirts
BATAS DE BAÑO		12.00	BATHROBES
CALCETINES		2.00	SOCKS
PAÑUELOS		1.00	Handkerchiefs
PIJAMAS		7.00	PAJAMAS
CORBATAS DE ETIQUETA		3.00	Nechties Drees
CHALECOS DE ETI...		7.00	VEST DREES
		10.00	COATS
		9.00	TROUSERS
		15.00	SUITS
			LADIES
PIJAMAS		8.00	PAJAMAS
VESTIDOS		15.00	DRESSES
		7.00	WAISTS
		2.00	BRASSIERS
		8.00	Night Gowns
		12.00	KIMONOS
		3.00	DRAWERS
		3.00	STOCKINGS
		1.00	Handkerchiefs
		6.00	Underskirts
		5.00	GLOVES
		7.00	GIRDLES
			CHILDREN
PIJAMAS		4.00	PAJAMAS
VESTIDOS		6.00	...RESSES
BLUSAS			
CAMISETAS			
CALZONES			
TRAJES			

PASS... OFFICE
27 AUG 1970
LONDON

FIRST SECRETA...

à moins de prolong...
at...

...GOVERNMENT OF INDIA
भारत
महात्मा गांधी MAHATMA GANDHI
1869-1948
1 रुपया RUPEE
J. J. Patel
SPECIAL SECRETARY, MINISTRY OF FINANCE

SERVICIO DE 1...

BEST IN THE PACIFIC
TONGA
THE FRIENDLY ISLANDS
POSTAGE
10s

BLUE GUM
15c
AUSTRALIA
CARD

MENU

蟹肉粟米
Crab-Meat With Sweet-Corn Soup

吉列蝦球
Fried Fresh Prawns

煎焗龍蝦
Baked Lobster, Onion Sauce

炒飯
Fried Rice

蟹肉芙蓉
Crab-Meat Fu-Yung

吉列石班塊
Fried Garoupa, Fish, Sweet & Sour Sau...

生果
Fruit

中國茶
Chinese Tea

MENA
HOUSE
PYRA...

BAGGAGE CLAIM TAG
№ 194026